MARTIN LUTHER KING JR. DAY

by Robin Nelson

first step nonfiction

Lerner Publications Company · Minneapolis

We **celebrate** Martin Luther King Jr. Day every year.

January

Sunday	Monday	Tuesday	Wednesday	Thursday	Friday	Saturday
		1	2	3	4	5
6	7	8	9	10	11	12
13	14	15	16	17	18	19
20	21 Martin Luther King, Jr. Day	22	23	24	25	26
27	28	29	30	31		

This holiday is in January.

Martin Luther King Jr. wanted
to make the world a better
place.

He saw that black people
were treated **unfairly.**

King dreamed that people of all colors would work together.

He tried to change **laws** in
a **peaceful** way.

Some people didn't like
what King was trying to do.

In 1968 King was shot, and he died.

People wanted to
honor King.

In 1986 we celebrated the
first Martin Luther King Jr. Day.

On this holiday, we learn
about King's life.

We also learn
about his dream.

People go to parades.

Choirs sing.

On Martin Luther King Jr. Day,
we remember King's dream.

We try to make the world
a better place.

Martin Luther King Jr. Day Timeline

January 15, 1929
Martin Luther King Jr. was born.

1964
King received the Nobel Peace Prize for his peaceful work.

August 28, 1963
King gave his "I Have a Dream" speech during a march in Washington, D.C.

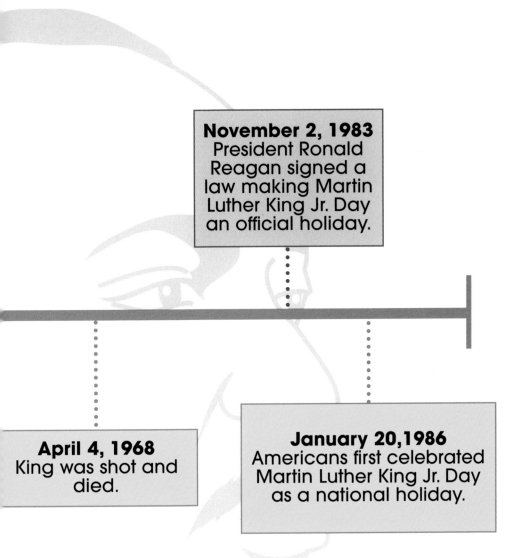

November 2, 1983
President Ronald Reagan signed a law making Martin Luther King Jr. Day an official holiday.

April 4, 1968
King was shot and died.

January 20,1986
Americans first celebrated Martin Luther King Jr. Day as a national holiday.

Martin Luther King Jr. Day Facts

 More than 27 countries all over the world celebrated the first Martin Luther King Jr. Day on January 20, 1986.

 Every Martin Luther King Jr. Day, schools, government offices, post offices, and banks close. These businesses close to honor the holiday.

 Martin Luther King Jr. Day was the first new holiday since 1948. In 1948 Memorial Day was created.

Martin Luther King Jr. is the only American besides George Washington to have his birthday as a national holiday.

 It took 15 years to make Martin Luther King Jr. Day a national holiday.

 Martin Luther King Jr. went to jail 29 times while fighting for the freedom of others.

Glossary

 celebrate – to have a party or special activity to honor a special occasion

 honor – to show special respect for

 laws – rules that people agree to share

 peaceful – without fighting or violence

 unfairly – not treating everyone in the same way

Index

The photographs in this book are reproduced through the courtesy of: © Flip Schulke/Corbis, front cover, pp. 4, 8, 16; © Bettmann/Corbis, pp. 2, 7, 22 (second from bottom); © Todd Strand/ Independent Picture Service, pp. 3, 12, 15; © Schomberg Center for Research in Black Culture, p. 5, 22 (bottom); SW Productions/PhotoDisc Royalty Free, p. 6; © Raymond Gehman/Corbis, pp. 9, 10, 22 (second from top); Courtesy of Ronald Reagan Library, p. 11, 22 (middle); © Carol Simowitz, pp. 13, 22 (top); © Morton Beebe, S.F./Corbis, p. 14; © Ryan McVay/PhotoDisc Royalty Free, p. 17.

This book is available in two editions:
Library binding by Lerner Publications Company, a division of Lerner Publishing Group
Soft cover by First Avenue Editions, an imprint of Lerner Publishing Group
241 First Avenue North
Minneapolis, MN 55401 USA

Website address: www.lernerbooks.com

Library of Congress Cataloging-in-Publication Data

Nelson, Robin, 1971–
    Martin Luther King Jr. Day / by Robin Nelson.
        p.   cm. — (First step nonfiction)
    Includes index.
    Summary: An introduction to the work of Martin Luther King Jr. and the day celebrated in his honor.
    ISBN: 0–8225–1282–3 (lib. bdg. : alk. paper)
    ISBN: 0–8225–1319–6 (pbk. : alk. paper)
    1. Martin Luther King Jr. Day—Juvenile literature. 2. King, Martin Luther, Jr.,
1929–1968—Juvenile literature. [1. Martin Luther King Jr. Day. 2. King, Martin Luther, Jr.,
1929–1968. 3. Holidays.] I. Title. II. Series.
E185.97.K5 N42 2003
394.261—dc21   2001007836

Manufactured in the United States of America
1 2 3 4 5 6 – AM – 08 07 06 05 04 03